THE BASICS OF BEGINNING BEEKEEPING

HOW TO START, MANAGE, AND HARVEST HONEY FROM YOUR HIVE INCLUDES MANY DIY BEEKEEPING TOOLS

DAVID NASH

Copyright © 2019 by David Nash

All rights reserved.

No part of this book may be reproduced in any form or by any electronic or mechanical means, including information storage and retrieval systems, without written permission from the author, except for the use of brief quotations in a book review.

PREFACE

Since you are reading a book on self-reliance, I am assuming you want to know more about how to take care of yourself in disaster situations

I would like to suggest you take a moment and visit my website and YouTube channel for thousands of hours of free content related to basic preparedness concepts

Dave's Homestead Website
https://www.tngun.com

Dave's Homestead YouTube Channel
https://www.youtube.com/tngun

Shepherd Publishing
https://www.shepherdpublish.com

PART I
ESSENTIAL BASICS

1
WHY KEEP BEES

Personally, I had wanted to get bees for a long time, but I was afraid it was too hard, or I would get stung too much.

After a little research an seeing how important bees are to agriculture and how valuable they are I decided to try my hand at beekeeping. For me it has been a very fruitful journey and I haven't been stung so much that the honey and wax have not made it worthwhile

In addition to using honey on my peanut butter sandwiches, Honey is also a great replacement for sugar, useful for wound management, seasonal allergy prevention, as well as using the pollination of the bees to increase my garden yield.

It stores indefinitely, and I found out, you can use it to make alcoholic beverages.

Besides, bees are indispensable to modern agriculture. Without bees to pollinate crops, we starve to death.

Plusses everywhere, beekeeping sounded to me like a win-win situation. The only think keeping me back from keeping bees was my wallet, and my relationship with my new neighbors.

When I started beekeeping all I knew was that there are two types of hives, the traditional langstroth hive everyone is familiar with (white boxy thing on a concrete block) and a top bar hive. (cheaper and easier but produces less honey and more wax as well as taking more knowledge).

I also knew that in my state, Tennessee, you are required to register and get a bee keeping license. The license was free and I applied, even though I cannot get my new bees until the spring. I will spent that winter loading up on all the toys, building my hives, reading, and most importantly, making sure my wonderful wife is on board with another project.

The following chapters cover all I learned in that year and the following 7 years as I became a better beekeeper.

2
SMALL CELL OR REGULAR BEES

The beekeeping association I am in is very much into small cell bees. As far as I can tell this is a concept first discussed by Michael Bush of bush bees. He has a very detailed page on the benefits of small cell bees, but as I have always only kept small cell bees I am not an expert on the subject. (I highly recommend all beekeepers read his book.)

However, I will tell you a little about the difference and why I keep the smaller bees.

First off, the large honey bees kept by traditional beekeepers are 150% larger than "natural" honey bees. This was done intentionally as the larger bee and the requisite larger cell in a honey comb produces more honey.

However, the issue is a parasite called a varroa mite. Varroa mites are external parasites that attack both honey bees and their brood. The mites suck the blood from both. This weakens and shortens the bee's life. Emerging brood may be deformed with missing legs or wings. Untreated infestations of varroa mites often kill colonies.

6 | THE BASICS OF BEGINNING BEEKEEPING

Brood Comb with Larva

Small cell bees create smaller brood cells, this means they can cap them much faster. The mites develop on bee brood. A female mite will enter a brood cell before it is capped so it is sealed in with the larva.

While inside the cell with the larva, mites will feed on the maturing bee larva. By the time the adult bee emerges from the cell, several of the mites have become matured, mated, and are ready to begin the process in other bee cells.

Since small cells bees cap brood cells much faster, this is a method to help control infestations.

Chemicals are also available, but I try to limit my beekeeping to more organic methods whenever possible.

At the risk of over simplifying it is more mite resistance or more honey.

It was a simple choice for me, especially starting fresh.

However, since most bees are kept in 5.4 mm cells, commercial foundation is made in that size. Natural cell is size is from around 4.6 mm to 5.0 mm. If you buy commercial foundation that is not labeled small cell, then the bees will probably grow to fill the larger foundation. If you have established bees and you want to regress them to the smaller size you need to make them build new comb. Repeating the process over several breeding cycles will shrink them back to normal.

In a new hive, with small cell bees purchase, just let them make their own comb without foundation.

I bought my bees as small cell bees, and purchased small cell foundation. It has worked well for me.

3

TOP BAR OR LANGSTROTH HIVES

When I decided on beekeeping I wanted to build my own hive. I had decided on building a Kenyan hive or a Top Bar Hive. This type of hive was designed by missionaries and aid workers in Kenya because of the simplicity of design. It is popular because it is a much more natural way of beekeeping. Additionally, it is thought that if the bees can build their hive how they want to, then they will naturally do what is needed to prevent beetles and mites.

It only took me a couple hours to build my hive body. However, I was stuck for months on figuring out how to make my top bars. This was because my shop tools are limited.

Additionally, I wanted to get the bee space right (bee space is the crawl space between comb 5/8 inch is ideal), but was having a hard time finding wood 1¼ inches to 1⅜ inches thick to account for the depth of the honey comb.

I solved my problem by buying replacement frame top bars for traditional Langstroth hives. My TBH was the same width as my langsthroth hives.

Kenyan style Top Bar Hive

Top Bar Hives are Simple and Cheaper than Traditional Hives

Besides the TBH being simpler, its cheaper, and I get more freedom with design. It's also easier to store because I leave it outside. I don't have extra frames and boxes to trip over all winter.

Collecting the honey is also simple because there are no frames so you cannot use an extractor. You are forced to either make cut comb or crush and strain honey as a harvesting method.

My mentors (who raise bees commercially) are fans of Langstroth hives. They are quick to point out that you get less honey with a TBH. That is because each time you gather honey you have to destroy the comb. This causes the bees to have to make more comb.

The process of building comb uses up many pounds of honey per pound of wax. Of course, that is not a problem for me. I want the wax. I have several candle molds. Beeswax also makes great bullet lube for reloading.

One thing to note is that TBH comb also has to be handled gently as there is no frame to hold it in place. If you are not careful it will break off and fall.

You Can Design Your Own TBH

All you need is a box, a way to keep the box off the ground, top bars, and a cover to keep rain out of the hive. I used a Kenyan design with sloping sides rather than a Tanzanian hive with vertical sides. This is because I have heard the bees don't like attaching comb at angles. This means that once you cut any attachments free it stays free.

Having sloping sides works just like the slightly sloping sides of an automatic firearm round, once it begins to move out of position, you get a lot more room to work so removal is a lot easier. If the sides were vertical, I would have to worry about bumping the comb against the hive the entire time I would be lifting it out.

Typical Langstroth Hive

Consider Both Types of Hives

You can expect yields of 50-60 pounds of honey from a Langstroth hives in a good season, a similarly sized TBH will yield less. But you will get much more wax.

For many years I ran both types, but currently I just keep a couple Langstroth hives in my yard.

4
ESSENTIAL TOOLS

You don't need a lot to get started, but there is some expense.

Beehive

A beehive is basically a series of wooden boxes without tops or bottoms. These boxes are called hive bodies and come in two basic widths and three basic depths

10 frame or 8 frame

This is the width of the body, it refers to how many removable frames of honey comb can fit in the box.

Most commercial beekeepers use the older 10 frame styles so this sized box is the easies to find. I prefer 8 frame bodies for several reasons:

- The are much lighter when filled with honey
- Because it is smaller, bees can heat them up an evaporate the water from the honey faster making them produce more honey
- 8 frame boxes are slightly cheaper
- It is more natural as bees like small spaces.

As to depth, your choices are shallow, medium, or deep.

Deep Bodies

Deep supers are 9 5/8" deep.

Deep frames are 9 1/4

Approximately 60 pounds of honey when all comb is drawn out and filled.

A hive will need at least one deep full of honey to survive the winter. Two deeps are kept on the hive at all times so the colony has room to breed.

Medium bodies

Medium supers are 6 5/8" deep.

Medium frames are 6 1/4"

Approximately 40 pounds of honey when all comb is drawn out and filled.

Three deeps are the equivalent to two deeps as it relates to creating space for bee larva.

Shallow Bodies

Shallow supers are 5 3/4" deep.

Shallow frames are 5 1/2"

Approximately 30 pounds of honey when all comb is drawn out and filled

They are typically only used for producing honey. I personally have never used a shallow.

While some mix and match, I find it easier just to stick with all medium bodies.

In addition to several hive bodies you will also need at a minimum:

Outer Cover

- Top cover. Also called a telescoping cover as it fits over the top five body like a cap on a telescope. It protects the hive from rain and the elements.

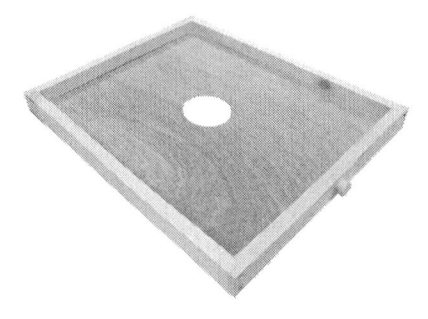

Inner Cover

- Inner cover. This cover is the same width and length of the bee box itself. It fits directly on top of the topmost hive body and the outer telescoping cover fits over it. It provides an additional entrance and acts as a moisture barrier.

Bottom Board

- Bottom Board. A bottom board is a section of exterior grade plywood with rails the hive bodies can sit on. It keeps the hive off of the ground and prevents rot. Mine is screened, which means that during the summer, and trash, dead insects, or mites can fall through the mesh keeping the hive much cleaner.

Frame with Foundation Attached

- Frames. The necessity to use removable frames is as much a legal requirement as a tool to help beekeepers harvest. A removable frame allows the bees to have something to attach comb to besides the top and sides of the hive. Most beekeepers insert sheets of beeswax foundation to help the bees build the comb size that the beekeeper prefers

This is the essentials of a hive, feeders, entrance reducers, queen excluders, and all sorts of additional items are available, however, for your first year, I would stick with the basics.

No matter what you pick, apiarists will tell you that you should always strive to keep at least 2 hives. In that manner you can use the stronger to help provide honey and possibly bees to supplement the weaker.

Hive Tool

Hive Tool

A hive tool is probably your most essential piece of equipment. Bees seal their hive and glue things together with sticky propolis. This requires you to be able to pry the hive open, cut and detach comb from hive sides, scrape propolis, and pry frames. I typically use one similar to what is pictured and a large flat head screwdriver.

Smoker

Bee Smoker

Smokers help a beekeeper by calming bees down. They aren't calmed as much as that it causes them to gorge on honey so they are lethargic. I did not always use a smoker, but I got tired of being stung and learned to use one.

Protective Gear

Full Bee Suit minus the gloves

To me good gloves are the most important, with a veil coming in a close second. My long-suffering bride however, won't do anything without a full suit. Bees don't want to sting, as they will die. However, if you move to fast or start accidentally smushing them they will sting to defend the hive. Because of pheromones, if one stings you other will. It is not uncommon to have 50 or 60 stingers stuck in my gloves when I get impatient while working with my bees.

Bee Brush

Bee Brush in Use

Some consider a bee brush an essential piece of gear to gently brush bees off of frames as you inspect. I have one, but I never use it. I just gently shake them off or blow them off the frame.

5

WHERE TO PUT YOUR NEW BEEHIVE

It is important that you set your hives in a location that was healthy for the bees. You also need to realize you will be working with heavy boxes of honey, so think about what is convenient for you. Also on my list of concerns was that the bees were sited in a way that did not bother my neighbors.

Sunshine Was My Biggest Concern

The number one concern of mine was that the area received good sunshine. This is because shaded colonies have more mites (http://www.ars.usda.gov/research/publications/publications.htm?seq_no_115=154678)

I wanted my hives to be in a well drained area to keep down mold, rot, and bacteria. For convenience, I also wanted the hives close to the house. This meant I could keep an eye on them daily. It also meant that I would not have to carry heavy supers of honey farther than I needed.

I Worried About the Neighbors

If you are an urban or suburban beekeeper I imagine you want to pick an area that will cause the least amount of disturbance to your neighbors.

When bees leave the hive, they tend to fly in a straight line. This means you need to put the bees in a spot where they are not directly in front of your neighbors. A solid fence it would force that line to be above the neighbor's head.

You can buy a warning sign, however, many states have laws to protect beekeepers from liability from stings as long as that beekeeper follows establish beekeeping practice. When I got my bees a particularly ignorant neighbor called the police and wanted be arrested for keeping bees. After a quick discussion with the officer and showing him my state's law on apiaries he spent some time educating the neighbors.

I have a video in the back of this work that shows more on how I sited by beehives.

6
HOW TO KEEP YOUR BEES OUT OF YOUR NEIGHBOR'S POOL

As an "urban" bee keeper it is very important to take steps to also be a good neighbor. Which means, sooner or later you will have to learn how to keep your bees out of your neighbor's pool.

Having bees can cause trouble in the neighborhood if your bees are constantly drowning in your neighbor's pool, or trying to drink the sweat off of your neighbor's neck while they are mowing.

This is a pretty common complaint, and one I had to deal with during the first months of my beekeeping adventures when a neighbor showed up on my doorstep one fine Saturday morning demanding I get my bees out of her bird bath.

I understood her concern, and assured her I would work on the matter. It is a simple fact that bees need access to fresh water. In the summer they literally work themselves to death flying millions of miles bringing nectar back to their hive.

If you do not provide the water, your bees will find their own supply. It does not have to be complicated; a bird bath will work as long as you have something in place for the bees to land on so that they do not drown in the water.

Bees Like Mineral Water

However, just like many people would choose a cool sports drink over warm water bees have their preferences, and given the choice between plain water and the mineral filled sweat of your neighbor, bees will take the mineral water.

If you have two neighbors with pools, and one uses a salt water system, and the other uses chlorine, bees are attracted to the salt water.

If we realize this, there are some additional steps you can do to enhance the water you provide.

I learned the following tip from our state apiarist during a lecture on Tennessee regulations on bees, and how to help your bees coexist in a neighborhood.

How I Kept My Bees from the Neighbor's Pool

A small animal mineral block, like the ones used in rabbit cages, can be used in your bird bath. It gives the bees some added nutrition.

What I did was take a small stainless steel bowl filled with water, planted the salt block right in the bottom of the bowl.

Then I balanced a strip of rabbit cage screen in the bowl. That keeps them from drowning. The bees can perch on the screen and have access to the water.

I put this bowl at about waist height about 20 feet away from the hives.

I routinely refill the bowl, and replace the block as it is depleted.

Finally, I haven't had any more complaints, and I can watch my bees drink from the bowl I supplied.

7
HOW TO PAINT A BEEHIVE TO MAKE IT LAST

The problem with Langstroth hives is that they cost money, and being wood in order to protect your investment, you need to spend time Painting and Sealing a Beehive if you don't want to keep buying new.

Knowing how to paint your beehive will protect it from the weather and make your expensive investment last longer.

I paid a little under $300 for two complete hives from a local beekeeping supply store.

How I Seal Paint Beehives

As $150 is a lot to spend on big wooden boxes, so I paint them to maximize the life of exterior parts. The first thing I do is to seal all the nail and staple holes, along with the end grain of the wood with a silicon sealer.

I use "White Lightening" 100% silicone sealant, and use my fingers to rub it into the cut portions of the wood. If you have a hard time finding it, tell the clerk at the hardware store that you need something without additives because it is bees. I was surprised that my clerk knew exactly what was needed when I said that.

The sealing part is not very hard, but it is a little messy.

The next day, after the sealer dried, paint the boxes with an exterior grade latex paint. I use white, for no other reason than I normally have white paint on hand. It has been said that white paint helps keep everything cool. However, in my experience bees don't care what it looks like, as long as there is no paint on the inside of their home. There have been studies on hive colors and it may make a difference, but I just don't get that far into it.

I have read that you should use oil based paints, and other places say to use latex paint. This is not something that I am worried about it. If you are worried about VOC in paint, prepares your boxes in winter and let them dry and aerate during the long winter months.

8
HOW TO ASSEMBLE LANGSTROTH FRAME BEEHIVES

Assembling Langstroth frame beehives is a simple process, but it can be tedious. I like getting the wife involved and doing this on an "assembly line".

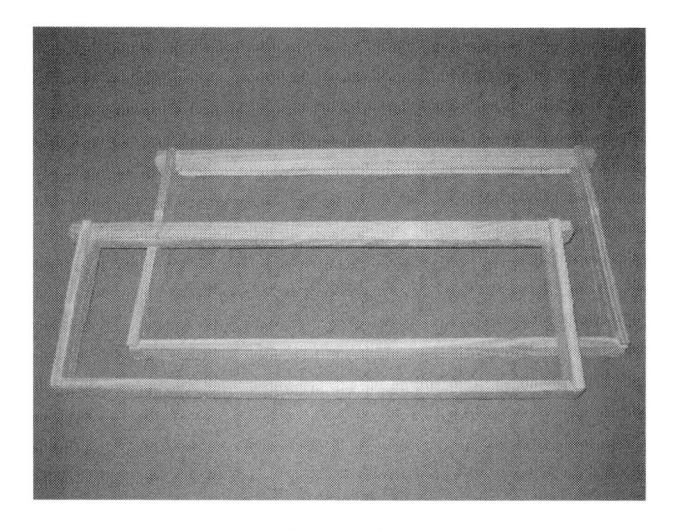

Typical removable Frame

Once your supers are painted, you will need some frames to put in you super.

There are three main sizes of frames, and they need to correspond with the size of your supers.

You do not have to assemble your own frames, they do come assembled, but the cost is greater. My supplier charged $1 a frame kit, and $1.75 per assembled frame. Since I was buying 50 frames, I obviously chose to DIY.

Each frame consist of a top bar, 2 end sections, a bottom bar, and 1 inch and 1 ¾ inch nails.

I also used some Titebond III waterproof wood glue. This was recommended to me as strong waterproof glue that does not bother the bees.

The only tools I used was a q-tip to spread the glue in the tight spaces of the end sections, and a small hammer.

Assembly of the Beehive Frames

Consistency is the key, you need to do it the same way for each frame, as the end sections are identical, but must be installed differently depending on they are left or right side.

The top bar also has a scored end for installing foundation, and that needs to always be installed the same way.

Personally, I lay out 8 frames at a time (since I use 8 frame supers) with each top bar facing the same direction, and then complete the same step on each frame before continuing with the sequence.

I also make sure I lay out all my tools in the same spot so I don't get my different sized nails confused, or my end pieces reversed.

1. Place top bar upside down on work bench, with scored end facing away.

2. Place glue on ends of top bar where the end sections will slide into.
3. Push end sections onto top bar, taking care not to twist sections as they are thin and will crack.
4. One side of the end piece will be flat, the other rounded. I always put the rounded facing me on the right side, and the flat facing me on the left.
5. Place glue in slots on end sections that will hold the bottom bar.
6. Insert bottom bar into slots on end sections.
7. The bottom bar has a precut slot running lengthwise. This should face the top bar, as the foundation will sit in this slot.

Nailing the Frames Together

1. Take the 1 inch nails and with the top bar sitting solidly on your bench, nail the bottom board to each end section.
2. Turn the frame on its side, brace the frame on your workbench with the lip of the top bar hanging off the side. Using the longer nail through the end section into the non scored side of the top bar. – Repeat for other side
3. Flip the frame so that it is sitting upright on its bottom bar, as it would hang inside the super. Once again using the longer nails, nail down through the top bar into each end section.

There are other ways of nailing the frames, but this allows for a strong connection that is not that difficult to remove if you later need to replace the bottom bar.

You will also need to take a utility knife and run it down the scored end of the top bar to remove that sliver of wood. This is can insert your wax foundation at a later date.

I have not added my foundation at this time because suppliers will refuse to ship the wax when it is cold, as the foundation is very fragile when it is chilled. I did not buy it earlier, as I don't want wax moths to eat it, so I will order it toward the end of the month and install it inside the house and take it outside when I get my bees.

You don't HAVE to use foundation, but it gives the bees a head start. If you don't use foundation, then the bees will not make as much honey. This is because much of the honey will go toward making wax.

HOW TO INSTALL BEESWAX FOUNDATION IN FRAMES

It is not technically necessary to put a foundation in your frames. Bees are perfectly capable of building their comb without it, however, there are benefits of using a good foundation.

While Not Necessary, Foundation Means More Honey

It takes somewhere in the neighborhood of 7 pounds of honey to make one pound of wax. Consequently, by installing foundation in the frames, the bees have a good start on making their comb. This allows them to store more honey than they would if they did not have the "head start". Bees use more resources to build wax than make honey. Some beekeepers believe bees build comb faster on foundation-less frames than they do on waxed foundation.

When I started out I deferred to the knowledge of those teaching me and have enough foundation for the first 3 medium hive boxes. This is what the bees need to eat during the winter. Once they get their food.

Additional Benefits of Using a Foundation in Your Frames

Foundation, especially the crimp wire foundation I choose to use helps give strength and stability to the comb. Greater strength allows honey extraction by the use of a spinning extractor so the comb to be reused.

Reusing honey comb will increase the size of next year's honey harvest. Without the reinforcement wired frames give the comb, spinning honey extractors cannot be used, so the crush and strain method of honey extraction must be used. Foundation also is especially needed in the Southern U.S. as heat will soften the wax and sometimes the comb partially melt and collapse from the frame. Foundation, (especially the crimp wired foundation) helps the comb resist the heat.

Why I choose to Use Foundation in my Frames (most of the time)

I decided on foundation in my frames because:

- It lets me get more honey per pound of nectar, so I can ensure the bees store enough to last the winter
- It makes a stronger comb that I can reuse so next year I have an even better harvest

Installing the wax foundation inside the frame is pretty straightforward; however, there are several methods we will discuss for KEEPING the foundation inside the frame,

Procedure:

1. If you have not already done so, cut/snap out the pre-scored "wedge" from the top bar of the frame.
2. Lay the frame on your work surface with the wedge side up.
3. Gently lift a single wax foundation sheet from the pile,

making sure to pull off the paper that keeps it separate from the others in the pile.
4. Gently (I keep saying that word, but you will see why when you buy foundation) insert the edge of the foundation in the grooved bottom bar.
5. If you are using crimp wired foundation, make sure the crimp wired end is at the top bar end, and the crimp is facing up, allowing the foundation to rest inside the top bars cut out section where the "wedge" once was.
6. Reinstall the wedge into the top bar, so that the crimped "L" shape of the wires are between the top of the wedge and the top bar, and the wax portion of the top of the foundation is between the side of the wedge and the top bar.
7. Gently, tack the wedge to the frame. I use a brad driver instead of a hammer, and place one small brad in the center of the wedge upward into the top bar, and a singe brad on each end of the wedge.

Embedding the Beeswax Foundation

Once the foundation is installed, you need to do something to keep the center from softening in the heat and collapsing. On the side bars of most commercially bought frames will be two small holes. The most common way of keeping the wax foundation inside the frame is to place wires through the holes across the frames.

If you are going to use wire to hold your foundation in place, you will need to place small brass grommets inside the holes so that the taut wire does not rip out of the soft wood. The wire need to be tight against the foundation. Attached the wire to the frames tightly. Next embed it into the wax. There are two methods of doing this. You can either use electricity to heat the wire so that it melts into the foundation, or you can use a spur embedder.

A spur embedder is a small toothed wheel attached to a handle. The embedding wheel is rolled over the wire. This action pushes the wire into the wax. A spur embedder is cheaper, but messier, and you have to be careful not to stray off the wire.

You Can Heat it

An easier, if more expensive way, is to use a short burst of electricity to heat the wire. Commercial electric embedders are available, but some use a electric train transformer. This method is easier and faster, but you must take care not to over charge your wire or the heat can cut through the foundation.

I choose a more DIY route, and used a trick I learned at the NABA bee school. Instead of messing around with wire, I bought a couple hundred bobby pins, and simply inserted a bobby pin in each hole and made sure they gripped the foundation between the two legs of each pin. A single frame uses 4 bobby pins, and is able to be completed in this manner both cheaper and faster than either of the two wired techniques. I like this way as it takes no additional tools, but I do worry about the bees build foundation around the pin as it does not sink into the foundation as with the other methods.

10

HOW TO INSTALL PACKAGE BEES IN A LANGSTROTH HIVE

A beehive is nothing without its bees, and while you can get "free" bees by catching swarms, its much easier to buy your bees. I like buying package bees because I have a reputable source. I want to be sure of what I am getting. If I collect feral bees there is no telling what diseases or pests will come with them.

I typically order my bees in January, so that the producer would have time to breed a queen for my package. This is one hobby that if you snooze you lose. If you do not order your bees then all the suppliers of package bees and queens will sell out by April.

Start With Two Hives

As mentioned earlier, it is best for a new beekeeper to start with two hives. I normally buy three-pound packages of bees.

There are around 4000 bees per pound. Consequently, I get somewhere between 10,000 to 12,000 bees in each package. These bees are of differing ages. A bee's job in the colony is tied to its age. Some of the bees will die of old age during shipping.

Construction of the Package

The package is a wooden box with two steel mesh sides. If you get your bees in the mail, it's a good idea to inform your post office. They like to get your bees delivered to you pretty quick. The buzzing can be unsettling for non-beekeepers....

On the top of the box, there is a wooden cover. That cover in over the top of a metal can that contains the sugar water that feeds the bees while they are confined. Also stapled under this cover is a strap that is attached to the queen cage.

Your bee supplier should be able to give you a good estimate of when they plan to ship you your bees. I know I bugged mine quite often as I was really enthusiastic about getting my first hives started. I prepared for the bees so that I could get them started as soon as they arrived.

Preparing the Hive:

The first thing you need to do is to set up your hive. I prepared mine a week in advance. In reality, a couple days should be sufficient lead time.

You want to make sure that your hive is in a sunny location. Ensure that the entrance is slightly tilted to prevent rain from running into your hive. It is better to provide frames that already have drawn comb in them so that the bees don't have to make the comb before they start growing and collecting honey.

Unfortunately that is not always possible for new beekeepers. Using frames with foundation is the next best step, and while it is not essential, you may want to lightly spray your foundation with sugar syrup. This will aid them in drawing comb. I did not do this with mine, as I was unaware of it at the time.

We discussed hive parts in a previous chapter, but to recap, you will need the following:

Hive Parts:

- Hive Stand (commercial stand, cinder blocks, wood boards, It doesn't matter as long as the hives are held off the ground, and are sturdy.)
- Bottom Board
- Entrance Reducer
- Feeder (entrance or interior) Not strictly necessary but it really helps.
- Brood Chamber: 1 Deep or 1 Medium Hive body (I use mediums for everything as its much simpler for me.)
- Brood Chamber Frames – 8 Frames for 8 Frame Hives, 10 For standard Langstroth Deeps and Supers
- Inner ventilated cover
- Outer Top Cover
- Weight for Cover (I used big rocks)

Once that's all set up and sited properly, your ready to install your bees.

Shake Out Method of Package Installation:

There are other methods, but this is the method I use. It is simple and fast. However, it does look scary as your shaking a couple thousand bees out of their box. It's easiest to do this in late afternoon on a day with little humidity as the bees are calmest then. You also should wear light colors as they get excited when big dark mammals mess around their homes. I think it's a genetic memory of big hairy bears munching on honeycomb, but my queens haven't confirmed that for me yet.

Procedure:

1. Remove three to four frames from the center of the hive

2. You may have "hitch-hiker" bees on the outside of the package. Gently brush them off with the back of your fingers, or your hive brush.
3. Remove the top cover from the shipping package with your hive tool or knife.
4. Using a knife or other tool, pry up and remove the can of Sugar Syrup from the Package.
5. Remove the caged Queen from the package (the Queen cage is shipped with either a strip of aluminum or wire attached. DO NOT remove the wire or strip)
6. Turn the package over with the opening directly over the top of the hive. Shake the Bees out of the Shipping Package directly into the frames.
7. Remove the Cork from the Candy end of the Queen Cage and using a nail make a hole through the candy which will aid the workers both inside the Queen cage and outside eat through the candy to release the Queen. The time it takes for the bees to eat through it is the time it takes for them to get used to the new Queen.
8. Using a thumb Tack or small nail, securely attach the Queen Cage to the frame which was previously removed with the mesh screen facing outwards between frames
9. I did not do this in the video. The method above has a higher Queen acceptance rate, and should be followed.
10. Replace the frame with Queen Caged attached make sure the Queen is facing outwards and facing the wax foundation.
11. Put back any frames that were removed from Step 1.
12. Replace inner and top covers
13. You can either discard the can (which is a waste), or you can open it up with a can opener and pour it into your feeders.

Leave Them Alone

The hard part is to leave Bees alone for at least a week. After a week open the hive to check if Queen has been released and laying eggs. If

Queen has not been released check to make sure Cork was removed from the candy end. If Cork was removed using a sharp object, dig out a hole in the candy to aid in the queens release.

Things to Think About

- Be careful not to damage the Queen.
- If Queen has been released remove the Queen Cage and close the covers.
- If the Queen has not been released check to see that the Bees are accepting the Queen.

This can be done by observing how the Bees are acting on the outside of the Queen Cage for aggressive behavior such as biting at the cage. Aggressive behavior is easy to see as the Bees will seem agitated and will move about quickly on the Queen Cage. Bees that are calm such as the ones in the picture below have accepted their new Queen. At this time the Queen can be released from her cage by removing the cork from the end opposite the candy. Replace the Queen Cage and let the Queen come out on her own, DO NOT try to remover her yourself. If the Queen has been released remove the Queen Cage and close the hive Covers.

All you need to do at this point is to monitor the hives so that you can add another hive body to the hives when they have drawn comb on all but the end frames. If you add boxes to early they can move up to the next body without drawing comb on the bottom box. Make sure they have plenty of food and let them do their business.

11

HOW TO LIGHT A BEE SMOKER SIMPLY

I want to give credit where it is due, I have spent a lot of time watching the "Fat Bee Man" on YouTube. This is my adaptation of his technique of how to start lighting a bee smoker.

The trick is to get a lot of smoke, but not a lot of heat. Which in my experience is not all that easy.

What you need is cardboard strips and either shredded paper, straw, burlap, or natural baling twine (I use commercial smoker pellets in mine because I use them in my BBQ smoker tube I use when I want to cold smoke something small in my grill, which is discussed in another book in this series The Basics of Cooking Meat).

Basically, you take a cardboard strip and roll it tightly and insert it in the smoker, it will unroll. Then top it off with some easily lit tinder. Light it, and blow air into the smoker by pressing the bellows. You should be able to hear the combustion.

Once it is lit and burning well, top it off with your fuel.

Lighting a Bee Smoker is a skill that takes some experience to master, but creating a cool smoke and using it appropriately is a skill every beekeeper needs to acquire.

I did not use a smoker at one time, but as time goes on I rely on it more and more. Over time, I decided I don't like getting stung.

Using a Bee Smoker

The rule for a smoker is less is more.

The smoke may mask the alarm pheromone and simulate a forest fire so the bees are busy eating honey, but it also disturbs the bees, and can contaminate your honey stores If you use too much.

A couple puffs of the bellows near the front entrance of the hive about ten minutes before you open the hive works well to start.

Use another puffs when opening the hive, or if the bees seem to be getting really upset.

Never hold the spout of the bee smoker less than 6 inches from the bees. The smoke is hot.

Do not set your bee smoker on top of or next to anything prone to scorching or melting!

12

PERFORMING YOUR FIRST HIVE INSPECTION AFTER INSTALLING BEES

An essential tool in your management toolbox is hive inspections. You need the ability to see what is going on inside your hive. Without that, you cannot make good decisions on what you need to do with your bees.

Now, if you are anything like me, you will be itching to dig inside your hive a few hours after you have installed your bees. I was excited to finally get started that I kept hanging out and hoping for a reason to check on them. However, you need to wait at least 5 days before you open your boxes up. Your girls need their privacy to get used to their new home.

Wait a Week at the Least Before Inspecting

Pick a day that is dry, sunny, and with little wind. Put on a bee suit, or at least light colored long sleeved clothing and a bee veil.

Set out all your tools. I use a bucket to keep it all in one spot. So I don't waste a lot of time while I am inside the hive.

I still need to find an inspection checklist to use for record keeping.

Unfortunately, I have not quite decided on what format to use, This time our main concern was to see if the Queen was released. Additionally, we wanted to practice finding her. Lastly, we were curious to see how much comb was drawn out.

Use a Smoker

The first couple times I used a. Smoker I had a hard time keeping it lit. I think it was the fuel I was using, but as long as it can be lit and is "smokey" it doesn't matter much what you use as long as its not toxic. You also don't have a "hot" smoke that will burn your bees.

I was careful to move slowly and deliberately. We approached from the side of the hive. Basically, we were sneaking up on them. Next, I refilled their feeders, and then opened the hive body.

If you are not careful of bee space when spacing the frames when you install your packages of bees you will get a lot of "burr comb" inside the hive. Bur comb is honey comb built where you don't want it, you should cut it out.

The Queens

Notice the Queen is larger and the bees defer to her

The main thing you are looking for on your first inspection is to see if the queen has eaten the candy plug in her cage and has escaped.

Look for your queen and see if she is laying eggs in the center of the middle frames, as she is supposed to.

Look to see if their is pollen, honey, and brood being stored in the combs.

Don't Rush

Remember to move slow and gentle and work from the outside in. This is something I forgot to do a couple times on the video. I put the frames in the empty hive body I put the feeder in; this keeps the frames off the ground.

If you rush to put extra hive boxes on your new hive before the bees have drawn out all the frames, they will "chimney" and start on the middle two frames in the upper box before they finish the outermost frames in the lower box. Don't rush anything, beekeeping is a marathon, not a sprint.

PART II
HONEY AND WAX

13
HOW TO STORE HONEY FRAMES BEFORE EXTRACTION

You need to ensure the bees have enough honey to last the winter, they need at least three medium frames of capped honey or two deeps of capped honey. Most beekeepers harvest the excess in the fall. I like to harvest in the spring and take what is left from the winter. However, you do it, sometimes you get frames of honey but don't have enough to make the cleanup of harvesting worth it.

It tends to take me a full weekend to extract, most of that being filtering and cleanup, and it seems that the cleanup is the same no matter how much I have extracted, so I don't want to got through the trouble for only a box or two

Store the Frames in the Freezer

What I do in order to easily undertake storing honey frames before extraction is to freeze the frames in my chest freezer.

I have found that my freezer's sides are the same size as the wings on my frames, so that the frames hang down naturally. I can fit about 2 and a half super's worth of frames in my little chest freezer and still shut the lid.

You may wonder about crystallization, but in my experience (and the experience of our state apiarist when I asked him), as long as you don't have repeated thaw/freeze cycles, it shouldn't be a problem.

Since I take the frames out of the hive, and keep them frozen until I extract, I have not have any problems with the quality of my honey.

The only caveat is that it does take some time to thaw the honey out and get it to a good temperature to flow in the extractor, so take that into consideration.

Otherwise, this technique has saved me a lot of trouble.

14
HOW TO EXTRACT HONEY WITH THE SMASH AND DRAIN METHOD

Normally beginning beekeepers don't rush out and buy an expensive rotary extractor.

For those without a rotary extractor, the best method of extracting all the sweet goodness from the combs is by using what is commonly called the "smash and drain" method. This method also works for those using foundation-less frames, or a top bar hive,

It's not brain science or rocket surgery. All you do is take the comb out, place it in a strainer and smash it up to break open each cell in the comb. Next you let it strain out.

If your using frames with foundation, you can take a spoon and carefully scrape the comb off the foundation. You might tear a little, but the bees will repair it.

Make Sure the Conditions are Right

You need to worry about humidity and temperature in the location you are extracting. The lower the temp the slower the honey will drain.

Additionally, the higher the humidity the more water the honey will suck out of the air.

Too much moisture will make your honey ferment. If your room is warmer than what is comfortable, your honey will drain a lot quicker, and you should be able to bottle it before you have any problems.

You also need to ensure your extracting room has screens on the windows or some other way to keep the bees out. Rather than fly to the millions of flowers it takes to make a frame of honey, the bees would rather just take the honey. I don't blame them, but I want my rent payment for their space in the yard so I try to keep them out of my house when I am extracting.

So this primitive method isn't hard, but it is less efficient than the extractor, and tends to be messier, however, for many beekeepers the cost savings is worth it.

15
HOW TO MAKE AND USE A DIY DECAPPING TUB

While I have a rotary extractor, I mostly use smash and drain honey extraction techniques. I do this because i find it easier.

Additionally, I want the wax as much as the honey, and because using homemade foundation, I end up breaking a lot of honey comb in the extractor.

I have been using a large tub, and just smashing the comb up and letting it drain out slowly, but the cheap plastic tub broke and I started looking for a new solution.

What I really wanted was the commercial honey decapping tub that I had been drooling over for a while, but at $129 dollars I figured I could do better.

Honey Gates for making a tub

In order to make my DIY Honey Decapping Tub I simply bought a large plastic tub, and some screws, a board, and a honey strainer. In total I spent under $50.

The most expensive part was the plastic tote, and the next was the honey gate.

Once I figured out where to bolt my frame rest, and drilled the hole for the gate, assembly only took a few minutes.

It was simple, I installed the honey gate on one end, and screwed a board across the top to give my frames a place to rest as I cut the comb off of them.

To use, just rest the frame on the board centered over the tub, cut out the comb and let it fall into the tub.

Smash all the honey comb up with a wooden spoon or other implement,

Let the honey drain out of the comb and then invert the tub slightly so the gate is the lowest point.

Open the gate and let the honey flow out into a bucket with a strainer sitting over the top to catch any bits and pieces of comb or bee parts.

16

HOW TO EXTRACT HONEY USING A ROTARY EXTRACTOR

Everything I have read suggests that I should extracting honey during the first week of September. That is the traditional time.

The way to tell if the comb is ready for harvesting is to look to see if the frame is capped with white tops.

Bees do not cap their comb until it is properly dehydrated enough that it won't spoil. Harvesting honey before its ripe and capped may cause fermentation and the loss of all your honey.

Have a Plan and a Place

If you want to be successful at extracting honey you need a plan. If you try to do this on the fly, your going to find yourself trying to extract before the honey crystallizes. You will also find that a good plan will help you from trying to find more bottles and equipment with sticky hands. This will help keep you from being lynched by your significant other.

Before harvesting can begin however the bees must be removed from the super. This can be done a in any number of ways, the most popular ways are:

- Using a bee escape
- Brushing the bees of the comb
- Using a mechanical blower
- Utilizing a fume board

I figured I could just pull a few individual frames out and brush the bees off. They did not like that and as they stung me repeatedly. I kept imagining a few instigators screaming "no taxation without representation! ".

Whatever method you use, you are going to need to have a closed place to put your frames. If your just removing full supers, then a bottom board and top cover will work. Since I just grabbed the first two frames I found capped, I used a Rubbermaid container and a lid. This was bought specifically to use as a decapping tub.

After you steal the fruits of your girl's labor your going to need an extraction area. It does not matter where it is as long as it is bee proof. If bees can get in, they will reclaim their honey. It is also very important that the area is clean. Additionally, It needs to be able to be cleaned easy. It *WILL* get sticky. You should have warm water available to wash your hands.

A Decapping Knife Helps

Cold Decapping Knife

I splurged on equipment and bought a special decapping knife. My budget did not allow the electric hot knife. It was around 15 dollars. Alternatively, you can use a serrated bread knife.

It should not matter as long as it is thin, serrated, and long enough to cut the entire depth of frame. I don't claim to have the only method, but this is how I uncap my honey.

- First, I set a metal strainer on the sides of my decapping tub.
- Next, I then turn the frame and rest it on its side on the edge of the strainer.
- This lets me slide the knife down the front of the frame and cut the capping off into the strainer.

If the comb was built nice and deep by the bees, run the knife along the edge of the frame. The comb should cut off in big flat chunks. After I cut the cappings off I use a capping scratcher to brush open any cappings. I bet you could use a fork in a pinch. However, I opted to buy all the cool tools.

After cutting both sides of the comb off. Just let the frames drain into the tub until I have several frames uncapped.

A Rotary Extractor Makes Extracting Easier

There are many ways of extracting honey from the frames, but the way that I find to be easiest, and from what I have read the most effective, is to use a centrifugal extractor. While a good extractor can cost upwards of $500, I found a plastic 2 frame version for $150.

Once you have some de-capped frames you place them into a rack in the center of your extractor (they sort of snap in), you put the lid on the extractor and crank it to get the rack spinning. As you spin the frames you will seed the plastic sides of the extractor turn darker as the honey is flung out of the frames by the centrifugal force. Only the honey on the outer side of the frame gets extracted, so you have to flip it around and repeat the process so both sides gets extracted.

Once the frames were empty, put them back in the hive for the bees to clean and refill with honey.

Strain Out the Bee Legs

Pure honey is safe to eat without further processing. However, there are always some bee parts and junk in the honey that people find unappetizing. You should strain the honey before bottling. They make a strainer set that comes in gradually diminishing pore size so you can ensure your getting all the gunk out of the good stuff, but I think the price was too much for a first year budget so I want to tell you a cheaper way using a jelly strainer bag.

I have a bottling bucket that is just a food grade bucket with a "Honey Gate" attached at the bottom. The honey gate is just a large spigot with a gate at the front for shutting off flow. I put a strainer bag over the lip of the bucket and put the bucket under the honey gate of the extractor. As the honey flowed out of the extractor it was filtered by the bag and filled my bottling bucket.

For smash and drain, I have even filled the bag up with smashed honey comb and let it drip out into the same bucket.

Let your honey set out in the kitchen overnight to let the bubbles and such settle. Supposedly, if the room is dry some of the moisture in the honey will also be removed during this "ripening" and the flavor of the honey would be improved. I cannot speak to this. All I know is that the next morning, I put a baking pan under the honey gate of my bottling bucket to catch any drips, and I bottled 11 pounds of the finest honey I have ever tasted. Now, I am sure, that when you get your first honey, you will feel the same way, but my fresh homegrown honey was sweeter than any honey I have ever bought at the store.

Bottle Your Work

Bottling was easy, Use sterilized jars, and just open the gate up and let it pour slowly into the jar. As it fills up, shut the gate and let the honey drip down into the jar to reduce the amount of leakage and waste. Just like canning, used a damp rag to carefully wipe any spills from the mouth of the jar as you screw on the lid.

17

HOW TO MAKE A BEESWAX INGOT MOLD FROM SILICONE

I like using my beeswax for other things like candles or bullet lube. However, it comes out of the hive contaminated with larva cocoons, bee poo, and other dark nasty bits. I clean it I end up my melting it over water so the clean wax floats to the top. This is easily done using the DIY Solar Melter I will show later.

However, it is hard to sell large blocks of wax. To fix this, I bought some molds to make 1 ounce and 1 pound blocks.

The problem with this is that whoever makes these molds uses vacuum formed thermoplastic. This makes inexpensive molds, but they melt too easily. Obviously, that is a problem when dealing with hot wax.

I used OOMOO30 from Amazon to make a much sturdier set of ingot molds.

How to Make a Beeswax Ingot Mold from Silicone

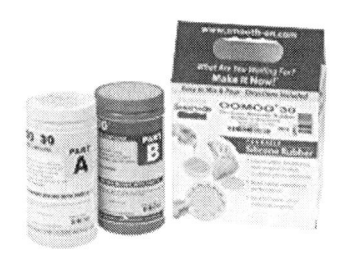

From playing with the OOMOO30 I found out how easy silicon is to use, and how well it handles hot wax. As a matter of fact, many candle makers prefer silicon molds to make candles. In experimenting I find it makes candle-making MUCH easier than my metal votive molds.

I figure if a candle mold can be made of silicon, why not a mold for making beeswax ingots.

All I did was pick my very best wax ingots to make molds from.

The better quality of product you use to make the mold, the better your mold, as any imperfections will be made into each thing you make in the mold.

I then glued them to the bottom of disposable aluminum baking pans. Like the foundation mold in the next chapter, I could have used a tighter fit between my ingots and the sides of the mold to make a more economical mold, but I wanted sturdy...

When I filled the pan with the mixed OOMOO30 silicon, and let it cure, I simply cut off the aluminum pan, peeled out the wax, and now have a perfect set of virtually unbreakable beeswax ingot molds.

If you want to do this to make votive candles, it is virtually the same process.

18

HOW TO MAKE A SILICONE MOLD FOR HOMEMADE BEESWAX FOUNDATION

This is a work in process, and is definitely in need of some refinement, but as I show it it works

I got into beekeeping for sustainability aspects. The idea of buying rolled beeswax foundation from an out of state supplier bothered me. However, it takes around 8 pounds of honey to make a pound of wax. Consequently, if you want to produce honey common thinking says you need to use foundation sheets and reuse your comb as much as practical.

The foundation is simply a sheet of beeswax that is embossed with the shape of the comb. Normally wax sheets are rolled flat in large steel rollers, and then rolled through rollers with the cell shape negatively embossed. Rolling the wax aligns the crystals in the wax so that it is not as brittle as sheets that are formed from dipping forms in melted wax.

When researching the idea of making homemade beeswax foundation, I quickly saw that with only 5 or so hives a 5 thousand dollar embossing machine was not practical. I did find a website that talked about making dipped wax sheets by dipping a metal or plastic sheet in hot wax several times, dipping in cold water, and peeling the sheet from the metal.

While this works, the sheet is brittle and you get a lot of breakage as you peel it off.

I wanted a mold. In some bee supply catalogs I saw silicon molds but they were $500.00 and they were for commercial sized bees. I run the natural 4.9 small cell bees, so if I wanted a mold I would have to do it myself.

Making a Foundation Mold

- What I did was make two mold boxes from scrap wood, and then glued a piece of small cell foundation in the center of each box. Remember that each side is different so ensure that you have each side represented.

- I used tape to build up the edges so that when I poured in the silicon it would make a flat sheet.
- Next I painted over the foundation and mold box with a silicon release agent.
- I used OOMOO30 from smooth-on and used the sample sized kit to save money.
- This silicon was very easy to use, I simply poured equal amounts of the yellow bottle (red liquid) with the contents of the blue bottle (grey blue liquid) and mixed thoroughly until mix was a uniform light purplish blue. Use something disposable as it is very hard to clean after mixed.
- Next, I poured the liquid into each mold box and let set.
- Once the silicon hardened (6-8 hours) I carefully pulled the silicon mold out of each box.
- Finally, I took the two silicon sheets and screwed them together to make the completed mold.

The bottom sheet was attached to a board to give some structure to the mold.

I could have saved some silicon if I had made the sheets thinner. However, I made them thick in the hopes of getting more use out of them. Hopefully, the extra weight helps spread the liquid wax more evenly.

DIY SOLAR BEESWAX MELTER

If you keep bees eventually you are going to have a lot of broken up pieces of wax to deal with.

Because I often use the crush and strain method of honey harvesting I have lots of wax to deal with.

Unfortunately my wax is is mixed with parts of bees, bugs, and other junk, as well as in chunks and pieces. I want to turn this into nice cream colored beeswax that I can both use and sell.

To turn ugly contaminated wax into pure wax you have to melt and strain it.

You can make a low cost simple diy solar beeswax melter using a garbage bag, an ice chest, and a pane of glass.

Because wax is hard to remove from the stove, my wife does not like me melting wax in the kitchen, but I am too cheap to buy a commercial solar beeswax melter.

This meant I had to improvise. I made something similar to what you would get in a hot car.

Materials:

- Styrofoam Ice Chest
- Black Garbage Bag
- Small container
- Water
- Cheesecloth or other straining material
- String
- Glass (cut to fit top of ice chest approximately 12×16)
- Optional Black Spray paint

Tools:

- 2 Hands
- Common Sense

Procedure:

1. Spray the inside of the ice chest black to help retain heat. It will make it hotter inside. (I did not want to modify the chest, so I just put a black Garbage bag inside.
2. Put ice box outside (somewhere it will get good sunlight during the day, but will not be knocked over or disturbed).
3. Place a small amount (2 inches or so) of water in your container. Th container should be heat resistant, I prefer glass or dark metal.
4. Place cheesecloth over the top of the container and tie it down.
5. Place container in the middle of the ice chest
6. Place wax in the center of the cheesecloth.
7. Put glass on top of icebox to act as a lid to retain the heat generated by the sun.

Over the course of the day the sun will heat the icebox (just like a car in a parking lot), which in turn will melt your wax. The wax will drip through the cheesecloth (filtering out bits and pieces of bees and bugs at the same time). This liquid wax will float on the top of the water, which makes it form into a block. Without the water the wax would solidify on the bottom of the container making it hard to remove.

If you repeat this process over the course of several days, I have heard that each pass through the solar melter will lighten the color of the wax. This is attributed to the filtering and the UV rays of the sun.

PART III

DEALING WITH PESTS

HOW TO USE POWDERED SUGAR TO CONTROL VAROA MITES

Varroa mites are an external parasite that can kill honey bees. It is one of the contributing factors in colony collapse disorder, as well as spreading viruses such as the deformed wing virus.

We use small cell bees as a method of controlling mite population as well as using a screened bottom board in out hives to allow mites to fall down and be removed from the hive.

However, we still need to check for mites in the fall before we close the hives for the winter, and there is a very simple method in using powdered sugar to control varoa mites

Equipment:

- Screened bottom board and chloroplast cover sheet
- Oil or shortening
- Sugar
- Flour sifter or mason jar with holes in lid

Procedure:

- Spread oil or shortening on chloroplast sheet, this will cause the mites that fall off the bees to stick to the board so that they can be counted. Insert this oiled sheet of plastic into the screened bottom board. Most have slots or runners already attached for this purpose. My supplier includes the chloroplast board with the bottom board as part of a set.
- Next you need cause the bees to groom the mites off of themselves, as well as reduce the mite's ability to stick to the bees. Powdered sugar does the trick as it is safe for the honeybees, stimulates grooming, and is a small additional food source. I used a helper to keep the flour sifter full of powdered sugar, as the bees got a little agitated as I sifted them with flour. But basically you open the hive and cover each box with powdered sugar.
- I check the board after three days to count the mites. If you do this in the fall and count 50-60 mites on your board you need to treat for mites using whatever method you are comfortable with. In the spring, the numbers are lower, as the mites will reproduce quicker because they prefer to reproduce in drone cells. In the spring treat for mites if you count 10 on the oiled board.
- Repeat as necessary, but not more than once every 10 days.

Note:

This is a meld of the two main ways to count mites, some insert the oiled board and do not add sugar. Others use the sugar in a mason jar and shake bees into the jar and then count how many bees have fallen off into the jar (I have attached this procedure as a pdf). My way is not standard, but it not only allows me to check for mites, but do a basic treatment at the same time.

21

HOW TO DEAL WITH WAX MOTHS IN YOUR HIVE

Wax moths won't typically kill a healthy hive, but they will not only kill a weaker hive, but they will make a horrible mess of your hive.

Not only will the moths damage your equipment they leave pheromones that will attract new moths after you have killed the old ones, so after you destroy the moths, wipe down your boxes, frames, and equipment with a 10% bleach solution to destroy the smell.

One good way to deal with wax moths, as well as prevent larva from taking hold, is to freeze your frames. Simply putting your comb in the freezer for a week to 10 days during the winter will do a lot to prevent infestation, as well as kill any eggs, larva, or adult moths. Once you have frozen your frames, store them where light can shine in, as this is also a deterrent.

You can also use moth crystals to kill wax moths and their larva. Just make sure you get a product that contains Paradichlorobenzene(PDB). Simply dump the crystals in a large heavy duty garbage bag, and then place the effected frames of comb in the bag, seal and let them fumigate for a month or so. Just remember to let any frames treated this way to be aired out for a month or so, as you don't want any remaining PDB to kill your bees.

One way or another, the best thing to do is to keep strong hives that can fight off wax moths. Keeping mites and hive beetles well controlled will do a lot to prevent moth infestations.

22

HOW TO MAKE HIVE BEETLE TRAPS

It is no surprise to most people that bees are dying, and some of the reasons behind it is starting to be better understood. Believe me, I am not an expert, but I do know that small hive beetles are a large part of the problem.

I bought some hive beetle traps to put in my hives. However, I want to start out with several options. My goal is to prevent the beetles getting a foothold in my hives. I spent a significant amount of money on my hives, so I don't want to see my work wasted because of an insect.

After seeing the commercial traps I realized that it was very simple to make my own DIY hive beetle traps.

The Best Use of a Political Sign

Basically, the trap is a short strip of corrugated plastic (think roadside political sign).

Cut the sign into strips about one inch wide and 3 or four inches wide. You want the corrugated strips inside the sign to run parallel with the short end making a long series of short tubes.

Rub vegetable shortening along one side to seal one end of the "tubes" and fill the open end with boric acid. Once the sign is filled with boric acid, seal the open end.

The way it works is that the beetles are attracted to the trap both because of the shortening and to get away from the bees that want to kill them as the intruders they are.

The beetles burrow into the channels in the plastic and are then killed by the boric acid. Its safe for the bees, as the channels are too small for them to get into.

The traps get stapled to the tops of a couple frames per hive body, and a few more get scattered around the top cover and the bottom board.

I made several more than I needed so that when I work the hive I have some with me so I can immediately replace any full traps.

This makes my life simpler as well as reducing stress on my bees by repeated opening and closing of my hive.

23

HOW TO MAKE A BEE SAFE PESTICIDE

I like to garden, and that means I have to deal with insects that like to eat my garden. Being someone interested in sustainable living I really don't like chemical solutions to my bug problem, additionally because of my bees – I cannot use pesticides without killing my bees.

After doing some research into a bee safe pesticide I found that a spray of Garlic will deter many of the pests eating my plants.

But I have some small fungal problems, and aphid problems so I decided to make a spray that had a few ingredients to deal with multiple problems at the same time.

To make this spray I simply bought the following:

- Garlic
- Denatured Alcohol
- Hot Peppers
- Spray Bottle

The procedure is pretty simple:

- Crush Garlic
- Mince Peppers
- Add both to a pot with a lid
- Boil in water until both the garlic and peppers are soft
- Process in a food mill (or alternatively liquefy in a blender
- You can strain this into a spray bottle and top off with denatured alcohol, but I dumped the entire mix in the sprayer and topped off with the alcohol. As I used the mix, I then was able to refill with alcohol, and get two more uses before the mix became too weak.

Since I have bees, I have to be careful when I spray. The mix won't kill the bees, but I don't want garlicky honey. Because of this I sprayed in the evenings, after the field bees went home for the night.

I had very good results with this mix, and I would love to hear your DIY garden mixes.

PART IV

NICE TO KNOW EXTRAS

24

HOW TO MAKE BEE FONDANT

Bee fondant is basically a sheet of hardened sugar candy that is used as a backup food supply to tide your bees over until they can start bringing in their own food.

If you are not greedy and leave the bees enough of their own honey to make it through the winter then you will not need fondant.

Some commercial apiarists use fondant because sugar is sometimes cheaper than honey. Fondant does serve a secondary purpose, in the winter months it helps absorb dangerous moisture that often kills colonies.

I looked over several recipes online, but in the end I choose the recipe from a local bee expert that has helped me tremendously when I was starting, Trevor Qualls from Bon Aqua Springs Woodenware. I listen to him because I respect his judgment when it comes to what is best for bees in my area, as well as he works to provide organic solutions to bee management problems. His recipe stays away from ingredients that are genetically modified, and I like that.

I followed his bee fondant recipe exactly, and it worked perfectly on the first try.

He does not mention it in the recipe, but the vinegar is used to invert the sugars to turn the sucrose in table sugar to glucose and fructose sugars found in fruits or honey. (This process is often used by those brewing alcohol also).

Trevor does say that the vinegar will not make your fondant taste like vinegar, and he is right about that. I broke off a little piece of the bee fondant to verify. It is very close to a piece of hardened plain sugar frosting. That is not surprising, because it is pretty much what fondant is.

Recipe for Bee Fondant

Ingredients

- Sugar
- Water
- Vinegar

Procedure

- Mix 1 part water to 4 parts sugar.
- Add 1/4 tsp. vinegar per pound of sugar.
- (Since 1 cup of sugar weighs 8 ounces. 8 cups of sugar needs one 16 oz. glass of water and 1 tsp. of vinegar)
- Bring to a boil, stirring constantly until boiling begins. (If you do not stir constantly you will get a transparent gel that is be extremely sticky instead of the opaque nonstick sheet fondant). The sugar mix will look clear.
- Boil covered for 3 minutes without stirring.
- Boil until mixture reaches 234° F. Take caution not to exceed 234° F as the sugar will caramelize and that is harmful to bees.
- Remove from heat and allow to cool to 200° F. This will cause the candy to have an increased thickness.

- Whip with a whisk until whiteness occurs.
- Quickly pour onto waxed paper having a towel beneath. Be sure that the towel is not fluffy since it will depress the cakes width. This method will make a nice cake.
- Allow to cool undisturbed.
- Remove wax paper and store each cake in a plastic bag in the refrigerator. The cakes can be handled as plates but may be a little soft like fudge. They will be completely white with whiter areas inside. Tiny crystals will shine from a broken edge.
- Place fondant directly over the brood cluster so the bees have access to it.

This is a very easy fondant recipe, but if you take care to not over rob your hives, you probably won't need it.

25

HOW TO MAKE AND USE SUGAR SYRUP FOR BEEKEEPING

Feeding bees sugar is one of those concepts in beekeeping that has a lot of controversy. It can cause as many problems as it solves. Consequently, I wanted to take a few minutes to talk about the issues in sugar syrup for beekeeping. That way, you can decide for yourself if it is needed.

Don't Take All the Bee Food

Honey is bee food. They make it so that they can store nectar to eat during the winter when there are no flowers. If you take all the honey during the summer you will have to feed during the winter so the bees will not starve. Historically (I mean pre-removable frames) beekeepers extracted honey in the spring-early summer and took honey from the year previous. This ensured that they only took the truly surplus. Modern beekeeping extracts in September and estimate how much to leave the bees for the winter.

Last winter was very mild. Therefore my queens started laying eggs early to build up numbers. All these new bees ate all the stores. When I went to check my colonies this spring I was shocked at how light they were with their stores. I had to feed to keep them from starving before flowers started blooming.

Easiest Way to Fee Bees is with Sugar Syrup

The easiest way I have found to feed my bees is to use sugar syrup. Sugar water is mixed in differing ratios depending on how it is used. Typically I mix 1:1 but sometimes I use a 2:1 ratio to make a thicker syrup. The water has to be fanned out of the mixture for the bees to turn it to sugar. This means a thinner mix is harder on the bees in humid weather.

Sugar water is sucrose. While nectar has fructose and glucose as well as minerals. This means sugar water is not as healthy for the bees. It also can lead to problems if feed at the wrong times or in the wrong ways.

You also want to stop feeding when you put on the supers you plan to extract honey from. I think it is dishonest to sell honey when it does not come from nectar. You may disagree, but I like honey not thick sugar water…

Honey Bound Queen

If you feed too much in the spring the bees can become "honey bound". This means that all the cells are full of food and the queen has no places to lay her eggs. This will cause swarming. Feeding too much in the spring can also cause the queen to lay too many eggs. That could cause a lot of death if a cold snap comes. The bees will try to keep the brood warm and may not move up into their supplies. It can also cause the colony to grow faster than their food supplies causing starvation.

84 | THE BASICS OF BEGINNING BEEKEEPING

Boardman Feeder on Hive Enterance

Something that has happened to me is that the supplemental feeding has caused some robbing. I use Boardman feeders because it is easy, However, all that sugar on the outside of the hive causes the other colonies to try to rob the hive, They fight for the sugar in their feeder and the syrup in the other colonies. This causes aggressive bees as they are very defensive of their hives.

A hive top feeder (without hive body and telescoping outer cover)

Feeding is best done inside the hive, That way you get less robbing. A hive top feeder is probably the best way to feed, Unfortunately, they are also more expensive.

Another Feeding Option

Another option is to put your solution in a plastic ziplock bag and cut some slits on one side. Place the bag on top of the frames inside your hive and the bees can stand on the plastic and get to the sugar water through the slits. I think this is really ingenious, but if you are clumsy it could result in a mess.

There are many other ways of feeding your bees. They all have some drawbacks. A simple internet search for feeding sugar to bees will give you a couple days of reading.

26

HOW TO MOVE A BEEHIVE

When I sited my hives, I was very careful to pick the best spot I could find on my property. As most beginners do, I made some mistakes. Not anything major, but my hives are just a little too close to a tree. This meant they get more shade than I like. If you make a mistake like I did, you may decide to move your hive. It seems very scary, but there is a process to do it successfully.

The general rule was to move a hive either 2 feet or 2 miles.

The idea is that if you only move the hive two feet, bees returning at the end of the work day will return to their home, not find it, and then start making larger and larger circles until they find it. With the hive 2 feet away from its original location, the returning bees would be able to find it very quickly.

Why you can't just move the hive

Have you ever moved to a new house, and after a long tiring day ended up driving on "auto-pilot" and found yourself almost at your old house? That's the idea of the 2 miles portion. Bees will take an orientation flight when they leave the hive and circle around and take note of where they live. They don't do this every time they leave, just when they first leave. If they haven't had an orientation flight after a significant changes to the area around the hive (or the hive location) they can get lost. As far as major mover, the theory is (as I understand it) is that when you board them up in their hive and then drive around to the new location, they know they have been moved and reorient themselves.

Now the problem comes if you need to move the bees across your yard. Your yard is more than 2 feet, but is significantly less than 2 miles. I was taught was to move it incrementally, 2 feet every couple days. However, I have moved a lot, and each move was stressful. Each time I moved it cost me a lot more stress than I thought it would as I planned. No surprise that moving a hive does the same to bees.

When they get moved, it takes them a day or two to get back in the grove of honey production. If I moved them, got them all shook up, let them get in the grove, and then did it again, well let's just say, if I was them I would be ticked....

Basics of Moving a Beehive

I went to Michael Bush's website Bush Bee and looked at his ideas for moving bee's. Mr. Bush is well known for thinking outside the box and taking his knowledge of bee's and using it to solve problems in somewhat unconventional manners. He has a method to allow you to move your bees 100 yards or less and in a single move to cut down on stress.

What You Need to Move a Beehive

- You need your hives
- Normal beekeeping gear (smoker, veil, etc)
- Second bottom board (or board big enough to set your hive on)
- Third bottom board (or board big enough to set your hive on)
- Second lid (or board big enough to cover your hive)

- Piece of cloth large enough to cover a hive box
- A stick or old branch that will disrupt the flight of the bees leaving the hive.

His method is simple, and I kind of followed it in the video linked at the end of this work.

Stack your hive in reverse order.

You place your second bottom board on the ground next you your hive and put the top box on the bottom board. Next take the next box off your hive and put in on the second bottom board. Repeat until you get to the bottom box on your hive.

Put the lid on the last box, and the second lid on the next reversed stack of hives.

Move the hive.

Pick up the bottom board, last box, and lid and move it in one piece to where ever you want to put your hive. Remove the lid and cover the hive with the cloth. This keeps the bees calmer, but it also allows you to remove it when you come back with your hands full of hive box.

Force them to re-orientate.

At this time you want to put your branch in front of the new hive. This will force the bees to move around the branch In doing this they will realize something has changed and take a new orientation flight.

Hopefully as they leave the hive and work their way around the branch and take off they should circle around the hive in larger circles as they see where they live. Since you only moved them 100 feet or so they are in their "neighborhood" it doesn't take very long for them to orientate their mental map.

Because you have reversed your hive boxes next to your original hive, all you have to do now is take the top box, put the lid on it to keep the bees from flying up in your face, and walk it over to your new hive location, grab the cloth, and place the box on the hive. Replace the cloth and repeat until you're down to the last box.

Leave a box for field bees.

Leave that last box for any returning field bees. It should have a landing board, but if not prop up an end with a stick. Come nighttime, block the entrance, and carry the box to the hive location, and put your branch at that boxes entrance.

DO NOT TRY TO PUT THIS BOX ON THE HIVE IN THE DARK.

I have opened a hive in the dark ONCE, and won't do that again… They are very defensive in the dark, and if you open the hive up its pandora's box and they will crawl all over you to pop you with their stingers. In the daytime you can replace this last box on the top of your hive.

Remove all equipment from the old location and watch for clustering of bees that didn't read the memo about the move. If you get some field bees clustering, just put a hive box at the old location and repeat the last steps of the move. You shouldn't have to do this more than once.

Moving them is not complicated, and the video below shows some of this a little clearer than my explanation, but take into account this is stressful to them, and it may hurt their production for a couple days.

27

HOW TO USE A NUC AS A SWARM TRAP

Swarming is the biological method bee colonies reproduce. Most beekeepers work very hard to prevent swarming. However, in my experience once a hive decides to swarm, it's almost impossible to stop them.

While swarming does reduce the numbers of bees in a hive (which reduces honey production). If you can catch the swarm you end up with a new colony.

Fortunately, that colony is predisposed to producing lots of comb.

My problem lies with my commute to work. Even if someone noticed one of my colonies swarming; I most likely would not be able to get home in time to catch them.

To deal with this I researched techniques for luring and "trapping" bee swarms.

How I Modified the Nuc Body to Make a Swarm Trap

I made a few non-permanent modifications to a nuc hive box and placed it in a tree

How to Use a Nuc as a Swarm Trap | 91

There are lots of commercial swarm traps available, However, they all seemed flimsy and lacking in longevity. The most popular seemed to be a pressed cardboard "flower pot". I don't have any personal experience in using that device. My thought is that it would not survive year to year.

For my trap I decided on using a wooden nucleus hive. I bought a complete nuc hive for $25.00. That is more than double the cardboard trap, but it has lasted me nearly 7 years.

I painted and sealed it just as I do all my wooden hive equipment. But to use it as a swarm trap I needed to mount it downwind of my hive and at least 8 foot above the ground.

The White Box in the tree is my nuc box swarm trap

What I ended up doing was using some galvanized steel plates to lock the hive body to the bottom board. I then screwed the entire hive to a section of plywood.

Next, I left enough room that the outer cover could fit on the hive body without having the plywood mounting board interfere.

I also drilled a hole in each end of the mounting board so that I could thread a ½ nylon rope through one end. The hole was small enough that the knotted end of the rope would not pass through it.

Before mounting the new swarm trap in a downwind tree, I put in 5 frames with new foundation in the nuc. I also added some lemongrass oil to the inside of the hive to attract scout bees.

I used pharmaceutical grade essential oil, as it is much purer and stronger than cosmetic grade oil. A few drops on the end of a q-tip were enough to properly scent the hive. I then ran the q-tip in and "X" pattern on the inside walls of the hive body.

Mounting Was Harder Than Construction

To attach to the tree I climbed a ladder and looped the rope a couple times around a suitable tree. By passing the free end of the rope through the other hole in the mounting board and then knotting it, the weight of the swarm trap put enough tension on the rope to hold itself up in the tree. This works just like a prussic knot.

My plan is that any scout bees sent from whichever hive of mine is planning on swarming will smell the lemongrass and be attracted to my nucleus hive. Finding a brand new hive body with pretty new foundation will cause him to report the swarm trap's location to the rest of the bees, and they will choose the easy option and move about 20 feet away from their old hive to set up shop in my bait hive.

I can then easily climb the ladder, untie the nuc, and lower it to the ground.

Due to the solid construction of my nuc hive, I plan on "forgetting" it in the tree until I notice a swarm has taken up residence.

Basically it's a $25 gamble to eventually earn a "free" colony. Since package's of bees are $75 and going up, I think it's a worthwhile endeavor.

PLEASE REVIEW

Please visit my Amazon Author Page at:

https://amazon.com/author/davidnash

if you like my work, you can really help me by publishing a review on Amazon.

The link to review this work at Amazon is:

https://www.amazon.com/review/create-review?asin=B07YGPBNSD

LINKS TO VIDEOS

The Basics of Beginning Beekeeping: Playlist

http://yt.vu/p/PLZH3jGjLQ0rD-1wZhbhKgYrrTLq_M9-Jq

Where to Put Your New Beehive

https://youtu.be/ncOAOt-SNBs

How to Keep Your Bees Out of Your Neighbor's Pool

https://youtu.be/Fw7lpXL4VWw

How to Paint A Beehive to Make It Last

https://youtu.be/q7PJHwDKl2M

Essential Seasonal Hive Maintenance

https://youtu.be/acql1RPJsXQ

How to Assemble Langstroth Frame Beehives

https://youtu.be/80ho3EF1Gp8

How to Install Beeswax Foundation in Frames

https://youtu.be/2dSlQWWrezI

How to Install Package Bees in a Langstroth Hive

https://youtu.be/YXZu7pmE8QQ

How to Light a Bee Smoker

https://youtu.be/1CD2TItEBeY

Performing Your First Hive Inspection After Installing Bees

https://youtu.be/4mURi_MDMlY

How to Store Honey Frames Before Extraction

https://youtu.be/Asb-llSr0Zk

How to Make a DIY Honey Comb Decapping Tub

https://youtu.be/uKBhaNS5_BI

How to Extract Honey with the Smash and Drain Tub

https://youtu.be/D7GwmB9ngmk

How to Extract Honey Using a Rotary Extractor

https://youtu.be/s283hHIeBCo

How to Move a Beehive

https://youtu.be/eK1QXFDGa5k

How to Make a Beeswax Ingot Mold from Silicone

https://youtu.be/AivAnLbkKbM

How to Make a Silicone Mold for Homemade Beeswax Foundation

https://youtu.be/CZrk-r0QUd4

How to Make an Improvised Solar Beeswax Melter

https://youtu.be/RGLQ3HrK3n0

How to Use Powdered Sugar to Control Varoa Mites

https://youtu.be/gMCF0Psaf9g

How to Use Garlic as a Varoa Mite Treatment

https://youtu.be/JSpKXY8twMs

How to Deal with Wax Moths in Your Hive

https://youtu.be/dq5SQq6667g

How to Make Hive Beetle Traps

https://youtu.be/_8qN0lOtuN4

How to Make a Bee Safe Pesticide

https://youtu.be/Ygm__CJakPI

How to Make Bee Fondant

https://youtu.be/Jn2yzZgLxq0

How to Make and Use Sugar Syrup for Beekeeping

https://youtu.be/OWLSR7YmYuk

How to Use Sugar Syrup for Beekeeping

https://youtu.be/fZWaoxxOEvM

How to Use a Nuc as a Swarm Trap

https://youtu.be/_qyfPKOyRD8

PRN Podcast Episode #18 Top Bar Beekeeping for Preppers

https://www.blogtalkradio.com/doctorprepper/2013/05/21/the-shepherd-school

BONUS: EXCERPT FROM THE BASICS OF
MAKING HOMEMADE CHEESE

The Basics of Making Homemade Cheese

Homestead Basics Book 4

David Nash

When I started my path to learning how to be more self reliant Cheesemaking and Soap-making appeared to be magical skills far beyond my meager abilities. Frankly I was a little scared to try them. Then, while cruising around the local home-brew/organic gardening store, I found a how to make mozzarella kit. I splurged and made my first homemade cheese.

It was wonderful. It was easy, and it was something that my wife was impressed by (of course I hid the kit)…

Seriously through, I found cheesemaking to be a great hobby. It is a rare skill that is alway a hit as a gift or something to take to a party. Like my other forays into DIY, this simple mozzarella kit grew out of control.

In this book I will show how to make farmhouse cheddar cheese, Yogurts, cream cheese, Ghee, Tofu, Seitan, DIY equipment, Rennet, and Cheese Cultures. I don't show the mozzarella recipe, as I don't want to cheat off of Ricki Carroll's Mozzarella and Ricotta Cheese Making Kit.

There are all manner of websites and classes for home cheese making as this is a great hobby, especially if you are a homesteader with a goat or a cow. However, few classes include bean based non-dairy like Tofu, Cultures, and DIY equipment in a basic class.

Don't think home cheesemaking is too hard or too expensive, It's much easier than you think. With some very simple ingredients and equipment (That I will show you how to make) you could be putting fresh, homemade cheese on your dinner table tonight.

Think of the joy of giving a homemade gift basket full of homemade cheeses, wine, and soaps all hand made by you with love, using instructions from this Homestead Basics Series.

If you like this Introduction to The Basics of Making Homemade Cheese, you can find it on Amazon.

ALSO BY DAVID NASH

Homestead Basics

The Basics of Raising Backyard Chickens

The Basics of Raising Backyard Rabbits

The Basics of Beginning Beekeeping

The Basics of Homemade Cheesemaking

The Basics of Making Homemade Wine and Vinegar

The Basics of Homemade Cleaning Supplies

The Basics of Baking

The Basics of Food Preservation

The Basics of Food Storage

The Basics of Cooking Meat

The Basics of Make Ahead Mixes

The Basics of Beginning Leatherwork

Non Fiction

21 Days to Basic Preparedness

52 Prepper Projects

52 Prepper Projects for Parents and Kids

52 Unique Techniques for Stocking Food for Preppers

Basic Survival: A Beginner's Guide

Building a Get Home Bag

Handguns for Self Defense

How I Built a Ferrocement "Boulder Bunker"
New Instructor Survival Guide
The Prepper's Guide to Foraging
The Prepper's Guide to Foraging: Revised 2nd Edition
The Ultimate Guide to Pepper Spray
Understanding the Use of Handguns for Self Defense

Fiction

The Deserter: Legion Chronicles Book 1
The Revolution: Legion Chronicles Book 2

Note and Record Books

Correction Officer's Notebook
Get Healthy Notebook
Rabbitry Records

Collections and Box Sets

Preparedness Collection

Translations

La Guía Definitiva Para El Spray De Pimienta

Multimedia

Alternative Energy

Firearm Manuals

Military Manuals 2 Disk Set

ABOUT THE AUTHOR

David Nash is a suburban homesteader with chickens, bees, rabbits, and a couple of goats in his suburban yard. For a while he even had an extensive aquaponics setup in his basement, until his long-suffering wife made him eat all the fish.

He knows how to raise animals humanely, simply, and without angering the neighbors. Dave runs a popular YouTube channel on DIY homesteading as well as being the author of several books on DIY preparedness and urban homesteading topics.

In fact, the tips shown in this book contributed to him receiving the third highest preparedness score on the TV show Doomsday Preppers

He is a father and a husband. He enjoys time with his young son William Tell and his school teacher wife Genny. When not working, writing, creating content for YouTube, playing on his self-reliance blog, or smoking award-winning BBQ he is asleep.

- amazon.com/author/davidnash
- facebook.com/booksbynash
- youtube.com//tngun
- goodreads.com/david_allen_nash
- twitter.com/dnash1974
- instagram.com/shepherdschool
- pinterest.com/tngun

Printed in Poland
by Amazon Fulfillment
Poland Sp. z o.o., Wrocław